TIG YOU'RE IT!

Also by Matt Beighton

The Shadowland Chronicles
The Spyglass and the Cherry Tree
The Shadowed Eye

**Monstacademy Series
(Ages 6+)**
The Halloween Parade
The Egyptian Treasure
The Grand High Monster
The Magic Knight

For Younger Readers
Spot The Dot

MATT BEIGHTON

TIG, YOU'RE IT

AND OTHER POEMS FROM THE PLAYGROUND

TIG YOU'RE IT!

Text and images copyright © Matt Beighton 2019

Matt Beighton has asserted his right under the Copyright, Designs and Patents Act, 1988, to be identified as the author of this work.

All rights reserved. This book or any portion thereof may not be reproduced, lent, hired, circulated or used in any manner whatsoever without the express written permission of the author.

Printed in the United Kingdom

First printed 2019

A CIP catalogue record for this book is available from the British Library.

ISBN: 978-1-9161360-1-4

www.mattbeighton.co.uk
www.greenmonkeypress.co.uk

For all the lost souls in the playground

THE CLASSROOM

Remember..3
Rhyming Is Dumb 4
Don't! 5
Parents' Evening 6
Terrible Facts 7
My Pet Dragon...8
Trip Day...10
Back To School..12
SATs...13

THE PLAYGROUND

Insults 17
Compost Boy...18
Your Game Is Stupid 19
Lost Souls..20
Last Day Of Term 22

THE BIG WIDE WORLD

A Trump..25
Painting...27
The Tiger Who Came To Dance.................................28
The Wind..30
The Elephant And The Dormouse 31
The Worst News..33
Ode To A Bogey! 35
My Days..36
Swimming Lessons 38

LONGER ONES

Technology..43
The Test...44
Battle For The Playground..46
Sally Saloo 48
Vest And Pants 51
Tig, You're It! 54
The Day The Football Died 56
Goldilocks...58

THE CLASSROOM

REMEMBER

"Remember capital letters!" she said,
"Remember your full stops,"
"Remember to join your letters," she moaned,
"And please, wipe up your snot!"

"Remember your fronted adverbials," she whined,
"Remember to use sub-clauses,"
"Remember to extend your sentences,
using commas to indicate pauses!"

"Remember semi-colons
and present perfect tense,
but don't forget to read it through,
to make sure that it makes sense!"

"Remember your written methods,
or to use your brain if you're able.
Remember to carry the one my dear,
and learn each of your times tables."

With all of that to remember,
I think I'm going insane,
With all of that to remember,
I think I've forgotten my name!

RHYMING IS DUMB

Why do poems have to rhyme?
I end up spending half my time,
finding a word that rhymes with sponge,
but I always end up with blancmange!

Why do poems have to rhyme?
Is it really such a crime,
if each last word stands on its own
lost, unmatched and all alone?

Why do poems have to rhyme?
For long enough I've toed the line,
so just this once, if it's all the same,
I shan't.

DON'T!

Don't go on the grass,
Don't go near the mud,
Don't play in the nettles,
And don't go near the woods.

Don't pick the flowers,
Don't play with sticks,
Don't run in the corridors,
And don't draw on the bricks.

Don't play British Bulldog,
Don't skid on your knees,
Don't wear fancy bracelets,
And don't climb up the trees.

Don't eat green yoghurt,
Don't wee on the seat,
Don't drink too much chocolate milk,
And don't eat bags of sweets.

Don't use your imagination,
Don't have any fun,
Don't take any risks at all,
Not any, not one.

PARENTS' EVENING

Kenneth is not the best listener,
he doesn't focus at all.
Sometimes when talking to Kenneth,
he just sits there juggling a ball.

He hates taking part in writing,
he isn't proficient at maths.
All he wants to do is eat bananas,
and he could really do with a bath.

I've tried everything in my power
to get Kenneth to stop and think,
but I think we need to accept here,
this isn't the best school for a chimp.

TERRIBLE FACTS

I learned some stuff in class this year
that made my stomach turn with fear -
from Henry's two beheaded wives
to soldiers fighting for their lives

We wrote about the dreaded plague
(a most wretched and unpleasant ague).
We read of people drawn and quartered,
and nasty pirates horribly slaughtered.

I read of a man with ten foot nails,
and countries that dine on garden snails.
We watched a woman wrestle a bear,
and found a spare pair of underwear!
(They went to lost property
in case you were wondering;
nobody claimed them
so now they're just mouldering!)

But by far the worst (this isn't nice),
worse even than Aztec sacrifice,
was the fact that my teacher picks his nose,
sticks out his tongue, and down it goes!

MY PET DRAGON

(To the tune of "I had a little brother...")

I had a pet dragon
His name was Bitey Pete
I put him in the classroom
To see who he would eat.

He chewed up all the children,
He gobbled up the staff,
He went for a nap,
Boy it wasn't half a laugh!

In came the doctor,
In came the priest,
In came the headmaster
Who'd had to call the police!

He burned up the doctor,
He burned up the priest,
He burned up the headmaster,
And we never saw the police!

TRIP DAY

All on time
And full of beans
No uniform
We're all in jeans

The amusement park
Or Cromer Bay
Buckle up
It's school trip day.

Permission slips
And first-aid kits
Two kids missing
They've got the squits

We're all lined up
The coach is near
We're out the door...

Of course we'll wait
For the fourteenth time
Whilst you have a wee
Rupert Grime

Off we go
We're back on track
We're out the door...

Inhaler Darren
I've told you twice
If you could listen up
That'd be nice

Off we go
We're moving fast
We're out the door...

Don't start to cry
What utter twaddle
Just be quick
Get your water bottle

You've left your bag?
Your coat's back there?
You've lost your bobble,
And tangled your hair?
How on Earth
Have you lost a shoe?
What a surprise,
You need a poo!

All worn out
And picking fights
We're finally off
Turn out the lights.

BACK TO SCHOOL

I lie awake and toss and turn
dreading what's to come.
At first they seemed to stretch away
those endless days of fun.

In my dreams the sun shone bright
and days were spent outside.
But all we got were overcast
and rain-filled leaden skies.

"We'll go to the beach!" Mum had said,
"A day at an amusement park!"
But all we saw were re-run films
eating popcorn in the dark.

I look back now as September dawns
and consider opportunities missed,
of pirate adventures or bike-ride-tig
and others, too many to list.

But next year I'll still get excited
after all, summer holidays rule.
But for now I'll lie here in darkness
because tomorrow, it's back to school.

SATS

Dreaded tests are looming large
with endless cramming sessions.
I've revised until I'm blue in the face
and practised my three point questions.

I've wandered around in bewilderment,
my long division is excellent,
I've learnt all the different conjunctions
and remembered how to spell ~~parla~~, ~~parle~~, government

I think I'm finally sorted.
A pass is on the horizon.
In a few more weeks it's over,
pending writing moderation!

The one thing my teacher told us,
that it's important for us to see,
the one thing the tests don't account for
is I'm amazing at just being me.

THE PLAYGROUND

INSULTS

Sir, she called me a poo-head.
No sir, he called me one first.
She said that I look like buttock.
He said that I smell like a horse!

Sir, he called me a flabtabulous frog.
Well she called me a baboon.
He said my feet smell like cheese, sir,
and that my head looks like a balloon!

Sir, I'm tired of being called moon-face
because my nose is unusually flat.
And I'm sick of being called hairball,
It wasn't me sir, it was my cat!

Listen up now to me both,
I want to make this perfectly clear,
you're both as bad as each other,
and I'm sick of your moaning, you hear?

You're both as mean as a hyena,
and as grumpy as a hungry bear,
so stay a hundred miles apart;
I think you'll agree that that's fair!

COMPOST BOY

There's this boy in our class
who lives behind the compost heap
and eats the rotten vegetables
and snores when he sleeps.

He always smells of lettuce
and old and mouldy bread,
his hair is always tangled
and matted to his head.

He wears a shirt made of cabbage leaves
with nothing underneath,
his face is covered in warts
and he's missing half his teeth.

The boy in our class, behind the compost heap
despite his many deficiencies, is quite nice, you see.
The best thing about this boy?
It's me!

YOUR GAME IS STUPID

                                                Shall we play my game?

No, play my game.

                                                Your game is stupid!

Yours is stupider…

                                                Yours is stupid times infinity!

Yours is stupider times infinity PLUS ONE!

                                                          …

                                                Well, your game stinks.

…

                                                Want to play my game?

Alright then.

LOST SOULS

We are the lost souls of the playground,
the kids who never make friends.
We're the terminally shy ones
whose loneliness never ends.

We've never had a girlfriend
or won the popular vote.
We don't speak up on the carpet:
our voices stick in our throat.

You ask us all to play nicely
and make a new friend every day.
But the playground is so big and scary
and we're never quite sure what to say.

We are the lost souls of the playground,
trapped in our solitary games.
We are the lost souls of the playground;
do you even remember our names?

LAST DAY OF TERM

Paper chains and festive cards
and endless silver glitter,
it's nearly Christmas time at last -
my brain is all a-jitter!

No more work for us to do,
even homework's out the window!
The teacher doesn't give a hoot,
unless he sees it start to snow!

We've sung our Christmas hymns in church
and watched Snowman on repeat.
We're filling up the hours now
with endless colouring sheets.

None of us want to be here,
but we're in it together it seems.
We're counting down the seconds,
to those snow-filled festive dreams!

Finally, the day arrives,
the last one of the year,
the holidays will soon begin
with presents, fun and cheer.

The teachers shove us out the door
(we hear them start to sing).
It's like they're glad to be rid of us.
But we'll be back come spring!

THE BIG WIDE WORLD

A TRUMP

If ever you find yourself feeling,
in a meeting or the middle of class,
that rumbling down in your tummy
of needing to let off some gas…

It's very important to remember,
that if you should relax and let slip,
everything here on this planet
eventually needs to let rip!

I bet you didn't know that The Queen
is a most terrible night-time pumper.
Sometimes the smell gets so bad,
the King covers his nose with a jumper!

The President of the United States
has a guff so obscene that it's felt
in every corner of the country
and that candles will often start to melt!

Even animals like to break wind
from an elephant down to a shrimp;
you should see the look on a gorilla
as his stomach swells up like a blimp.

He won't hold it in there for long,
he just closes his eyes and relaxes.
Sometimes the jungle starts steaming
with all of his noxious bum gases!

So remember, the next time you rumble
don't hold it in, that's absurd.
Just smile at the people around you,
and make it the loudest that they've ever heard!

PAINTING

There once was a girl in Class 3,
who was sharp and as clever as can be.
But when it came down to art,
she wasn't as smart,
because she painted her paintings with wee!

THE TIGER WHO CAME TO DANCE

The other day in our playground,
A tiger climbed over the fence
He wandered up the headmaster
And asked if he wanted to dance

The headmaster graciously declined
(He said it wasn't within his milieu)
So the tiger turned and asked us
If we knew a tango or two

I'd long been practicing my rhumba
My breakdancing, street and cha-cha
So forward I stepped
and snapped up my chance
With the tiger who'd popped by to dance

We did the Charleston, the Jive and the Tango
Even the Electric Bugaloo
We waltzed (Viennese and traditional)
And found time for a Salsa or two

We worked our way through the robot
Before finishing off with a foxtrot
But soon the bell chimed
And called end on my time
With the tiger who wanted to dance

THE WIND

There once was a boy from Torbay,
who would gurn something rotten each day.
But the wind changed its course,
now he looks like a horse,
and he's left eating bales of hay.

THE ELEPHANT AND THE DORMOUSE

The elephant and dormouse
are quite different indeed.
One's big as a house
the other, as small as a seed.

One has ears as big as the moon,
a nose that hangs to the ground,
a tail that swishes to and fro
and it makes an almighty sound.

When stomping through the jungle
or drinking from a lake,
you can always spot an elephant
by its trunk as long as a snake.

But the mouse is very different,
just between you and I,
it's very hard to spot, you see
and perhaps you're wondering why…

Its feet are soft and silky,
it barely weighs a pound
and when it scurries to and fro
it doesn't make a sound.

But as with every animal,
including you and me,
they're also very similar,
just have a look, you'll see…

Of ears, they both have two,
a pair of eyes to see,
a swishy tail, a nose to smell
and - I think you'll quite agree -
that though you and I are similar
our differences abound.
But that's just fine by me because
they make us fun to be around!

THE WORST NEWS

It was the worst thing they could say to me
surely, it couldn't be?
We were all sat down eating dinner;
my mum, my dad and me.

I should've known something was wrong,
that trouble was about to land.
My parents were giggling and smiling,
and holding each others' hands.

But I didn't pick up on the warnings,
not even when they started to whisper,
my mum just held onto her tummy,
and said, "You're going to have a sister!"

I swallowed my ice-cream and thought
this was all just one horrid dream.
Why would they drop such a bombshell?
Honestly, I just wanted to scream.

I knew what was coming, of course.
My best mate Tommy filled me in.
His sister was born before Christmas,
and they'd already forgotten about him.

They forgot when it was his birthday,
they never took him to the park.
They'd even stopped tucking him in at night,
and left him alone in the dark.

He had to give up his bedroom,
and throw away all of his toys.
His sister arrived like a comet;
an endless bundle of noise.

So as I sit here and write out this poem,
I'll definitely need to act soon,
there's only one course of action:
I'm going to have to go live on the moon.

ODE TO A BOGEY!

Oh bogey, how do I love you?
Let me count the ways…

The way that I can find you
yet you're never up there alone.
That I can roll you in my fingers
like a semi-precious stone

At times you feel like a mountain,
but you might be small and tiny.
Sometimes you're firm and crispy
and others wet and slimy

I love that I can flick you
or stick you underneath the seat,
but the way that I like most of all
is how tasty you are to eat!

MY DAYS

Life is such an adventure
When you're only two and a bit
I laugh, and roll and stand and crawl,
But sometimes I just sit.

I sit in the corners
Or on the windowsill
I sit inside my mummy's cupboard
Or behind my daddy's drill.

I wake up every morning
Ready to start my day
It doesn't matter where we're going
Mum and dad will lead the way.

Some days I go to nursery
And spend it with my friends
With ball pits, dragons and bouncy castles
And fun that never ends.

When each new morning comes, I open my sleepy eyes
And see my mummy staring down like she's won the biggest prize
She swoops me up into her arms and gives me a squishy cuddle
She sneaks me back into her bed for such a cosy snuggle

We crawl our way under the quilt
And tickle daddy's feet
We laugh and giggle and pretend to make
A den from all the sheets

Some days I go out walking
On adventures in the park
We'll take a picnic and lots of toys
And stay out 'til it's dark.

I get to spend a million hours
Playing with my grandma
With sleepovers and midnight snacks
And being treated like a star!

But when the sun goes down
And I lay down my tired head
I like to finish off my day
All snuggled up in bed!

SWIMMING LESSONS

Is there anything nearly as scary
as your very first swimming lesson?
"There're sharks in the water,"
your brother proudly boasts.
"Or piranhas," laughs your sister,
you're not sure which you fear the most.

Your trunks are too big,
your dad's hand-me-down,
he swears they were once in fashion
in beige and dark dingy brown.
Your goggles are still in the car,
and your towel is already damp,
from sprinting around the changing room
trying to avoid getting cramp

You snap the cap on your forehead
(after fifteen hundred tries).
There's talcum powder in your ears,
and chlorine in your eyes.

Your instructor's an ex-drill-sergeant

who shouts at you from her seat.
You always get given the float
that smells like sweaty feet.

You're forced to swim in the deep end,
and float around in your PJ's,
and fetch bricks of cement from the bottom
without any further delays.

There's nothing nearly as scary
as those horrible days in the pool.
Just remember that when you grow up
you get to make the rules!

LONGER ONES

TECHNOLOGY

We walk down streets with glowing faces,
Suburban zombies, tech disgraces.
Minds absorbed in glowing screens,
An infinite, silent, social scream.

Counting retweets, checking likes,
Important memes and hashtag might.
Endless mistakes and social stupidity;
Leading inexorably to cultural vapidity.

Always connected, never alone.
Who needs friends? You've got a phone.
No face-to-face or human contact
Just digital input lacking tact.

Click-bait links and fake-news streams:
A constant battle to define obscene.
Polished pictures filter-filled,
Our own self-worth #killed.

THE TEST

Silence falls, all quiet except for the boy at the back
who's lost his pencil and can't find his rubber.
Breath stuck in my throat,
"I only had one day to practise!" comes the cry of the fallen soldier.
The single sound - the second hand of the
classroom clock running down the time left -
before it all comes to pass.
The rest of my life
mapped out by the scrap of paper sat on my desk
so quickly torn from a notepad.

"Where is it? You had it last!" the teacher had cried
exasperated by my, once again, missing book.
"Dunno," I'd mumbled under my breath;
it wasn't where I'd left it, I knew that.
"Question one!" the teacher says shouting in the silence.
The quick shuffling of papers and pencils and curses of those who
- despite the warning sirens –
forgot to write the date.

Soon it's over, sweat beads on my forehead but at least,
I managed to answer them all.
Lauren passed out at question five and
Geoffrey had to race to the toilet and missed number ten.
There'll be a note in their bag, that's for sure.

We go out to break whilst the teacher counts up our score
but none of us can concentrate - football has lost its fun
and hide-and-seek is nothing more than 30 children
all hidden away behind trees lost in quiet contemplation
of just what is waiting for them on the other side of the abyss.

It happens.
The bells rings.

We take our seat as the teacher hands us back our papers.
Red ink, that's never good.
Two.
Two out of ten.
There'll be a letter in my bag tonight.
I hate speeling tests.

BATTLE FOR THE PLAYGROUND

We step out onto the playground,
Morning dew still damp on the grass.
We pick our side of the concrete
- You near the netball hoop, me by the swing -
Our eyes meet across the tarmac
Old foes ready to battle.

In the distance, the school gate creaks.
In perfect unity, like wolves at a new moon,
We howl our cry to all who'll listen.
"Who wants to play *my* game?"

Panic flashes across our classmates' eyes:
Tig or football? Football or Tig?
You get Billy, no surprise there.
I get Keith and Sally, ever reliable.
Arms around the shoulders of
Our new found compatriots,
Screaming together, we take up the cry;
"Who wants to play ***our*** game?"

They flock to us now, we rule the yard.
In ones and twos they join our banner
Eager to play; they're not sure who's playing what now.
But no matter, they join anyway.
"Who wants to play ***our*** game?"

Voices heard even on the big playground.
Younger kids startle at our noise,
But rally around us,
Sensing something bigger than them.
Finally it happens,
Balance, equilibrium.

We have enough people to play the game,
Though in truth we had enough before,
But, drunk on power, we kept recruiting.
No matter now though, we're ready to play.
First things first, sorting teams –
Eanie meanie miney mo…
Finally sorted…
Thomas quits…
"I thought this was Tig," he shrugs and leaves.

We grumble and moan but carry on,
The ball placed on the centre spot.
Ready to go…
The whistle blows, end of break…
I look across the playground,
And catch your eye.
We know what this means come lunchtime:
"Who wants to play *my* game?"

SALLY SALOO

There once was a girl called Sally Saloo,
Who couldn't have been much older than you.
She was taller than most, with shocking blonde hair
And went through the world without hindrance or care.

Often she found herself walking to and fro
Seeking adventure, or places to go.
It never did help that she knew east from west
She still ended up wandering lost on her quest.

Now one morning was different, last Thursday I think,
Her father was late and had caused quite a stink
About the fact he might miss a meeting or two;
Things like this never bothered poor Sally Saloo.

She waited in bed until it was no longer dark
And headed off out to Pampaloo Park.
The park had it all, from small ducks to a zoo;
So plenty of things for our hero to do.

But something was different this day, you'll soon see,
And it started whilst Sally was sat under a tree,
Minding her own business, she didn't like to seem brash,
When suddenly she heard a great bang and a crash.
It came from up high, in the bow of the oak,
From an old rusty lamp, all battered and broke.

Thinking quick on her feet, Sally shook the great wood,
Hoping to knock the thing down, if only she could.
But try as she might the thing just wouldn't budge,
And soon she was sweating and bearing a grudge.

She pulled and she yanked and she twisted and jumped,
She pounded it, kicked it, flicked it and thumped.
It wasn't until she gave one last great big tug,
That suddenly down came the rusty old jug.

From the lamp came a shout that made Sally fret,
"Rub me three times and three wishes you'll get".
She rubbed and she rubbed, though timidly at first,
And out popped a genie, quite obviously cursed,
For he stood not much taller than the smallest of mice;
About two inches point 3, if you want it precise.

"I'll grant you three wishes, not four and not two,"
Came the voice of the genie all tiny and blue.
"Though warning is needed fair maiden, I'll vouch,
That wishes I wish for don't often work out."

Not wishing to heed such a boring old warning,
Sally wished her first wish, to set sail before morning.
She yearned to be a pirate out plundering gold,
To raise a Jolly Roger on adventures untold.

But true to his word the wish didn't quite work out,
And caused our young Sally to splutter and pout.
The boat that she saw she agreed couldn't be finer,
But it turned out she was leaving on a holiday cruise liner!
Her days were now spent singing songs to old dears,
And prancing and dancing and drowning her tears.

Two more wishes she had, she knew to think hard,
Her journey so far had most definitely been marred
By his backwards wish making and his lacklustre skill,
But still she was seeking that adventurous thrill.

"I wish for more money than a king's ever seen,
I wish to be richer than the wealthiest queen."
A flick of his wrist and the sky rained down gold
But the money was foreign, quite useless I'm told.
She realised that this wish was perhaps not so wise

For the weight of the coin caused the ship to capsize.

Sally swam to the distant and desolate shore,
Sat down on her haunches and thought hard once more.
The third wish, she thought, must be better than most,
No money or sailing or self-centred boast.

She sat and she thought through rain, sun and hail
And came up with a wish that she knew couldn't fail.
The one thing she wanted, the thing she knew best,
Was to be back in a place where she knew east from west.

"Adventure is fine," she said to herself,
"So long as you know who you are in yourself."
"These wishes I've wished for, were greedy and wrong
And made me feel weak for not being strong;
I knew in my heart that despite several tries,
Adventure was near, if I just opened my eyes.
The book on my shelf or a game with my dad,
Are all big adventures just waiting to be had."

The moral of this story, if one can be found,
Is it's often quite easy to go looking around,
For adventure and mischief and to escape the mundane,
And those things are fine, every now and again.
But take a stern lesson from Miss Sally Saloo,
And don't wish things to happen, just get out and do.

VEST AND PANTS

When I was at school
My worst lesson was PE
Back then, we had to do
Every PE lesson in
Our vest and pants

It didn't matter if
We were doing gymnastics indoors
Or rugby outside,
We had to wear our vests and pants
We made quite the sight,
30 children chasing a rugby ball
All dressed in just our vests and pants

Of course, back then
Winters were colder as well
I remember once stepping outside
We were supposed to be running laps
But instead the playground had frozen
And so instead we played ice-hockey
In our vest and pants

It was so cold that we had to
Keep stopping play
To clear the penguins out of the goals
I remember once
Our teacher was sick with the plague
And instead we had a supply
Who came to teach us PE
Of course, in our vest and pants

Now this supply teacher
As cheap as I'm sure he was
Had us running scared
Right from the very start
He had an eye patch over his right eye
And a wooden peg for leg

I know what you're thinking
And so were we - pirate!
It didn't help that he had a parrot
That lived on his shoulder
The worst thing of all though
About our pirate teacher
Was when he taught us dodgeball

Our school was very poor and couldn't
Afford the correct equipment
"No need to worry!" the pirate had told the head
"I'll bring my own dodgeballs!"
And he did
A bag full of heavy, iron cannon balls
Left over from the Spanish armada I'll wager
He ordered us out into teams
Obviously, in our vest and pants.

A hundred children on each side
If my memory serves me correctly
You could barely move for nervous sweaty bodies
All trying their hardest to get
As far away as possible!
And all in our vests and pants!

The whistle was sounded
And pandemonium ensued
A thousand children all trying
To duck, dodge and hide from
The flying metal cannon balls

Only the oldest children were
Strong enough to lift the balls
And soon the weaker ones
Had been filtered out, stretchered off
And taken to the waiting ambulances.

I'd found the best way to survive though
Hiding beneath a wooden bench
At the back of the hall
Only my bare feet visible
But that was enough for the Pirate
"He's under the bench!" he cried
And suddenly the world exploded
As cannon ball after cannon ball
Thudded into the bench
Splinters flew from the floor
The sound was deafening

I knew I had only one option
A cowardly, last ditch option
I knew that I needed to surrender
To wave a white flag on a stick
Luckily I had something white
That I could get my hands on quickly
You should have seen
The horrified look on their faces
As I stepped
From underneath the bench waving
My hastily removed white flag hanging
From my raised fist

In hindsight, I should probably
Have used my vest!

TIG, YOU'RE IT!

Thump, thump, thump
My heart pounds in my chest
Thump, thump, thump
My breath comes shallow
Mist forming in the air
As I stare
Through a window lined with sticks
Out onto the battle field
Shadows flitting by
It won't be long now...

Thump, Thump, Thump
My heart echoes through my ribs
Thump, Thump, Thump
Eyes dry as I force them open
Not daring to blink
They'll even hear me think
About escaping
Running from this hide
It'll soon be time...

Thump...Thump...Thump
My heart slows down
Time is running out for them
I doubt they'll find me now

When suddenly from behind
Bursting through the trees
An arm
Pokes me on the shoulder
"This is it..." I surrender
A war cry fills the sky
"Tig, you're it..." he says
And leaves

Thu...
My heart stops beating
What's the point now
Outcast until lunch
Maybe even longer
Everyone will know
As we sit there in maths
That it's me, I'm "it".

As lonely as a single cloud
Or Thomas who picks his nose
I'm the only one on my team
And everybody knows

There's only one thing
Left to do
The honourable way to cope
With such a life changing catastrophe...

I'm changing schools tomorrow

THE DAY THE FOOTBALL DIED

I remember it like it was yesterday,
the way that it spluttered and sighed.
I remember it like it was yesterday,
the day the football died.

We'd all been taking penalties
(I scored, in case you cared)
when up stepped Skinny Simon
who was football-skilled impaired.

His touch was worse than an elephant,
he was lankier than a giraffe.
When he tried to control the ball,
we'd all fall about and laugh.

With every misplaced pass and shot,
we'd shout and scream and howl,
but as he shuffled forward
it suddenly wasn't funny now.

On this fateful Tuesday,
about mid-June, I think,
when Skinny Simon approached the spot,
my heart began to sink.

The ball was new and shiny,
it still had that new-ball squeak.
"This one's going top bins," he said,
"I'll knock it into next week!"

He took a moment to breathe,
we saw him stop and dwell,
the cogs were turning too slowly
and he stumbled, tripped and fell!

He landed elbows first,
such was his lack of grace
(it's since been said he was lucky,
he could have ended up on his face!)

His elbows hit the gravel
and he did a forward roll,
his bottom hit the football
and it shot towards the goal!

All of us were frozen.
Surely, it couldn't be?
Lanky Skinny Simon,
scoring the best goal you'll ever see?

But alas! It didn't happen,
the 'keeper punched it clear.
It bounced off at an angle
in the direction of Mr Mageer!

Now Mr Mageer was a teacher
with a most unfortunate nose.
It was long and thin and pointy
and prickly (like a rose)!

Normally his nose wasn't a problem,
though the hairs could do with a snip,
but right now it filled up the world
as the ball landed right on the tip!

Poor old Skinny Simon,
you should've seen the look on his face
as the protruding schnoz pierced the ball
and he was dragged away in disgrace

Football was banned for a year,
even though we shouted and cried.
I remember it like it was yesterday,
the day the football died.

GOLDILOCKS

I don't know if you were ever told
About the girl with locks of gold
Who often wandered in the woods
Rarely getting up to good
Instead she'd often run amok
She went by the name of Goldilocks

For miles around and then some more
They'd lock the windows and bar the door
They set alarms and rang the cops
As soon as they glimpsed her golden locks

But nevertheless she was never charged
And for many years remained at large
Breaking and entering and stealing things
Like grandma's knickers or ruby rings

The best policemen were often stumped
And would arrive to find they'd been gazumped
Or were just too late to foil her plot
She was out the window, had taken the lot

Once or twice they had her nicked
But nothing they threw would ever stick
And she'd always leave with a knowing smile
But they kept her DNA on file
A decision that would soon prove key
When it came to solving case 3B

One Sunday morning, just past six
The wench set out to get her fix
Of stealing stuff that wasn't hers
(She had her eye on her grandma's furs)

She was in the woods and on the prowl
When her pesky stomach began to growl
She wanted something warm and sweet
A tasty, yummy, sticky treat

She wanted it quick and time was tight
(There wasn't a fast food place in sight)
The only joint for miles around
Was a tiny cabin in humble grounds

With thoughts well suited to a vagabond
In through the door slipped our craven blonde
The first thing she thought was "They've got nowt
Except for a bowl of porridge oats"

But always one to beg and steal
The gal sat down and stole a meal
The first bowl was, she'd later cry
far too cold and way too dry

The second bowl, worse by far
Was far too hot and thick as tar
With options fading she came at last
To a one last chance to break her fast.

The final bowl was warm and sweet
And the devilish girl sat down to eat
She wolfed it down and licked the spoon
Afraid the owners'd be back soon

Feeling stuffed and slightly sick
She looked around for stuff to nick
The walls were covered in expensive art
The tricky part was where to start

But first things first, to put up her feet
She looked around and picked a seat
Once again, there were choices three
She pounced on one with girlish glee

The first was big and bruised her bottom
The next was broken, lumpy and rotten
The third of course was right on spec
And our fiendish girl thought "Blinkin' heck!
If I weren't here to commit a crime,
This seat would do me mighty fine."

In the end she up and tried
To find somewhere to rest her eyes
A trio of beds she found next door
"It's surely better than the floor?"

Of course you know how this bit goes
From bed to bed she had a nose
Before she finally settled down
On the smallest one in a dressing gown

It wasn't long before she learned
The owners of the house'd returned
Three gruesome and angry hairy bears
It's then our villainous girl despaired

As quick as a whip she fled the scene
The mess she'd left was quite obscene
She knew, if caught, it was jail for sure
Without a thought she was out the door

She didn't know but somewhere there
She'd left an errant golden hair
It was a perfect match for case 3B
To convict our girl of ursine larceny

The judge she drew was widely dreaded
And sentenced her to be beheaded
No later than dawn at the village stocks
And that was the end of Goldilocks

ABOUT THE AUTHOR

Matt Beighton is a primary school teacher from the middle of England. He has two young daughters who provide a constant source of inspiration and sleepless nights.

His unfortunate classes are often the test subjects for new stories and he feels that he owes them a debt of gratitude for putting up with some of the more terrible ones over the years.

If you have enjoyed reading this book, please leave a review online. Your words really do keep authors going!

To find out more visit
www.mattbeighton.co.uk

www.ingramcontent.com/pod-product-compliance
Lightning Source LLC
Chambersburg PA
CBHW040510110526
44587CB00045B/4239